The Immaculate Conception of the Blessed Virgin Mary

A Retreat

on
The Immaculate Conception of the Blessed Virgin Mary

Cadoc D. Leighton OPraem

Gracewing

First published in England in 2021
by
Gracewing
2 Southern Avenue
Leominster
Herefordshire HR6 0QF
United Kingdom
www.gracewing.co.uk

No part of this publication may be reproduced, stored in a retrieval system, or transmitted in any form or by any means, electronic, mechanical, photocopying, recording or otherwise, without the written permission of the publisher.

The rights of the literary estate of Cadoc D. Leighton OPraem to be identified as the authors of this work has been asserted in accordance with the Copyright, Designs and Patents Act 1988.

© 2021 Literary Estate of Cadoc D. Leighton OPraem

ISBN 978 085244 978 3

Typeset by Gracewing

Front cover:

Cover design by Bernardita Peña Hurtado

Contents

Contents..v
Foreword..vii
Opening Prayer..1
First Conference...3
Second Conference..11
Third Conference...21
Fourth Conference...31
Appendix..39

FOREWORD

 N A YEAR when the world experienced the ongoing effects of the Covid pandemic, our community—like so many families—struggled on whilst coping with the death of a greatly loved member of our religious family.

Fr Cadoc Douglas Auld Leighton was born in Bellshill, Glasgow on 28 July 1950. He was educated at Rutherglen Academy, Glasgow. After leaving school, he worked as the librarian for the Scottish National Opera Company. During this time, he met some of the confreres from the abbey of Kilnacrott who were working in the parish of Kilmarnock.

He entered the abbey of Kilnacrott and was clothed as a novice on 18 September 1976. He was professed on 8 September 1977 and ordained a priest on 1 July 1983.

He began his academic career at Maynooth, Dublin, in 1977. He graduated with a first class honours degree in Modern History and Greek and Roman civilisation in 1980. He then studied divinity and graduated with a first class honours degree in 1983. After this, he taught at the seminary for two years. In 1985, he went to the University of Cambridge to begin his doctorate. He graduated with his PhD in 1990. There then followed two years teaching at St Norbert's College, De Pere, Wisconsin. During this time, he was appointed visiting Professor of History at the University of Chicago.

In 1992 he spent two years helping at Maryvale College in Birmingham and supervised the first graduate students in the college in the field of Newman studies. In 1994 he became Professor of History at the University of Bilkent in Ankara, a teaching post he enjoyed until he retired in 2016. On his return to the UK, he was Parish Priest of Camborne and Redruth in Cornwall. Amongst his many distinctions and honours, Fr Cadoc was a member of the Cornish Gorsedh (he was proud to be a Cornish Bard) and he wanted to spend time in a parish hoping to use his spoken Cornish. He delighted in blessing the children in Cornish (much to their great astonishment).

After feeling unwell for some months, on Thursday 30 April Fr Cadoc was diagnosed with Metastatic Liver Cancer and the cancer had spread throughout his body. Fortified by the rites of Holy Mother Church, Fr Cadoc went home to the Lord on 1 May 2020, a First Friday dedicated to the Sacred Heart, the feast of St Joseph and the first day of the Marian month of May. This sums up his life and his priesthood.

As he received his last Holy Communion, Fr Cadoc greeted the Lord with the words, "Expecto te, Domine". He died as he lived, in hope and expectation of the Lord.

There is no one quite like Fr Cadoc, who has always been a faithful and kind confrere. His unfailing cheerfulness and his delight in the absurd was always a source of comfort and strength. His great love of snuff tobacco provided so many opportunities for the mortification of his confreres. He was always a man of strong opinions and forthright in his views. Yet, like Bartholomew in the gospel, he was a man completely without guile. His greatest desire is that we would remember him as a faithful priest and a true son of Mary Immaculate.

Amongst his many academic works is his book *Catholics in Protestant Kingdom*, a study in the Irish *ancien regime*. He also wrote extensively on Gallicanism and the veto controversy, the Irish manufacture movement 1840–1843 and also Non-Juror Anglican clergy. This led to the studies he enjoyed the most, the English Enlightenment and, more importantly for Fr Cadoc, the Counter Enlightenment. This was only some of Fr Cadoc's wide and extensive interest in all things.

It is a great joy to add now this publication to his list of many achievements. This retreat was transcribed (and all footnotes added) by Fr Stephen Morrison OPraem from Fr Cadoc's hand-written notes, in July 2020. The retreat was preached by Fr Cadoc in August 2011 in St Philip's Priory, Chelmsford, to the canons there assembled.

We remember it as one of the best community retreats we have experienced. We hope that you too will benefit from Fr Cadoc's wisdom, his love of the True Faith and his great devotion to our Blessed Mother.

We ask only in return that you please remember our beloved Fr Cadoc in your prayers.

In Christ and St Norbert,

✠ Abbot Hugh Allan, OPraem
25 March 2021, Solemnity of the Annunciation

Opening Prayer

Fr Cadoc began each conference with this prayer, written by the French Oratorian priest, P. Charles de Condren (1588–1641). It was given an indulgence of 300 days by Blessed Pope Pius IX on 14 October 1859. Fr Cadoc added intercessions to Our Lady and the Saints before the conference began, including to St Herman Joseph of our Order (see beginning of fourth conference), a special devotee of the Mother of God.

Jesu, vivens in Maria.

O Jesus, who dost live in Mary,
come and live in Thy servants;
in the spirit of Thine own holiness,
in the fullness of Thy power,
in the reality of Thy virtues,
in the perfection of Thy ways,
in the communion of Thy mysteries.
Have Thou dominion over every adverse power,
in Thine own Spirit, to the glory of the Father. Amen.

First Conference

ERMIT ME, PLEASE, to start out on this course of lectures comfortably for myself: allow me to talk of what I know about, to talk about *history* ... and recall Blessed Pius IX's sojourn in Gaeta in the winter of 1848–49. He had been driven from Rome by a liberal-nationalist regime which hated the Catholic Faith, and accordingly killed priests, as opportunity offered. Gaeta, just out of reach of the revolutionaries, in the *Regno*, in the Kingdom of Naples, is on the coast. Blessed Pius stood silently for a long time watching one of the storms that can batter that very beautiful coast in winter. Cardinal Lambruschini,[1] a very devoted servant of the old pope, Gregory XVI, stood by him and thought of the storm that beset the Barque of Peter. And at length said: "Most Blessed Father, you can heal the world only with a proclamation of the dogma of the Immaculate Conception." And so, it is

said, began the process which led, six years later,[2] to the proclamation of *Ineffabilis Deus*, which declared that, "the Most Blessed Virgin Mary, in the first instant of her conception, by a singular grace and privilege granted by Almighty God, in view of the merits of Jesus Christ, the Saviour of the human race, was preserved free from all stain of original sin."[3]

Now, I ask you not to reflect on the statement from *Ineffabilis Deus* that I have just read, but upon what is, as we hear it, that most remarkable statement of Luigi Lambruschini. And, if one reads his little book on the Immaculate Conception,[4] dedicated to another very faithful Marian priest and fellow member of the Sacred College[5], I don't think one can doubt that he meant precisely and literally what he said—and believed it with his whole heart. I add, that the events of those six years between 1848 and 1854 reveal that he was putting into words what the whole Catholic world believed—that the act of definition could effect a real and substantial change in the world. Our own Father Faber wrote, in 1855, a little pamphlet explaining the "Doctrine and Definition of the Immaculate Conception" to the Catholics of England—and he opened it with the words: "The Definition of the Immaculate Conception will probably be the greatest event of the nineteenth century. It will be an epoch in the history of the world..."[6] These words of Father Faber and of Cardinal Lambruschini were not hyperbole: and Catholics did not hear them so. I fear that most Catholics now would almost certainly do so, being unable to take them seriously; and that betrays a mind purged of a Christian perception of reality.

Think; here is Lambruschini, a practical statesman in troubled times, looking upon Europe's terrifying history during his adult lifetime—a Europe many of whose elites had acquired a contempt and hatred for Christianity—a Europe racked by murderous, genocidal revolution, blazing up into a new kind of war that enveloped whole populations and spread over the whole continent. And behind this, driving it, a sustained attempt to destroy the Christian Faith by the most *subtle* and the most *brutal* methods. And even after rivers of blood had been poured out to quench this fire, still Europe seemed to be possessed by disordered passions which called for a new order of institutionalised sin. The Revolution survived.

And the good Cardinal's response! It was not a political one; not a call for a renewed Catholic society with its instruments in government, in education, in the social order and the like. Yes, if you could have those things, good—and there were those trying hard to achieve them. But that was not the priority; for that reflected only an inadequate, human view of what needed to be done. And, then, if it was the Will of God that these afflictions were to lie on the Christian world…? No, what was to be sought was the triumph of Mary in the world, with an act of dedication to her. And that is what the Definition of the Immaculate Conception was seen as—that's what it was all about. After all, there was no raging dispute about this matter in the Church that needed settling. There never really had been; thought, debate, yes—but no conflict. So why define?

The answer lies in the truth that the clarification of doctrine is always an occasion of grace. This goes for each of us. *Knowledge* of Christ and Mary go together with *love* of them. And thus God does not thrust truth upon us; He does not overwhelm us with it, merely contradicting and confronting us. He *does* guide us into the discovery of truth, allowing us to appropriate it, and in such a way that it will be fruitful in our growth in love for Him. So it is with the Church. The definition was a declaration that the Church had understood more of the Revelation in Christ and would respond to that increased understanding with increased devotion to Mary—and grace is given most when it is sought, and cooperated with. The definition therefore was seen as a petition for an outpouring of divine grace, given through Mary's own hands.

The Church, in all its trials of the nineteenth century, was characterised—I am saying—by a quite visible manifestation of an internalised grasp of the primacy of the supernatural order. And we do need to recover that in the Church now, and in our life in the Order, and in our own lives. We need, if we are disciples of Our Holy Father Augustine, to keep our eyes fixed on the building-up of the City of God, and averted from the life of the earthly City, which is always going to remain meaningless to us. At a personal level, we need to be less concerned with the *external* circumstances of our own lives, and focussed on co-operation with God in the work of our Salvation. That is *why* we are on retreat.

Those who have gone before us, marked with the sign of the Cross, in the reign of *Beato Pio Nono*, had, I think, an instinctive and often articulated understanding that the *external* worship[7] of Mary here on earth was a matter of supernatural significance—that such actions, performed by the Church Militant on earth, constituted conformity to a supernatural order, one element of which was what we might call the Magnification of Mary—and thus of the Blessed Trinity—for her soul "magnifies the Lord."[8]

Mary, in contrast to her Son, *grew in grace* during her earthly life. Mary continues to *grow* in the *Church*—Triumphant, Suffering and Militant—and in the lives of all its individual children. In Heaven, love of Mary continues to grow in the love of the angels and the Redeemed. By their willing sharing in the suffering of Christ, by which He lovingly redeemed His Mother, the Holy Souls too experience greater love for Mary. On Earth, the greater devotion shown to Mary by the Church as a whole nurtures a magnification of Mary in the hearts of individuals—by increased love for Mary, increased faith in Mary, increased reverence for Mary, increased confidence in Mary, increased thanksgiving to the Holy Trinity, for Mary herself and for the gifts we receive through her. The historical phenomenon of increasing understanding of Mary and devotion to Mary over the centuries is but the tip of the iceberg. The whole will only be seen in the light of Heaven.

We are here[9] quite good in our expression of devotion to the Most Holy Mother of God. But we must ensure that that is grounded in supernatural motivation: a vision of reality drawn from Revelation by which we are constantly aware of Mary's activity, and constantly exploring it:

- Her *constant* bringing of Christ into the world—that continuation of her divine Maternity;
- The constant triumph over evil by the *Immaculata;*
- The constant thanksgiving to God—her existence as an oblation of praise, as the Church regards her in celebrating her Presentation;

- We might go through the life of Mary, reflecting on how the mysteries of that life are constant universal phenomena in the Church.

What hinders us from possession of this vision of the life of Mary all around us? Simply—it is the world; that world which is our enemy, but by which we are fascinated. We believe its deceit—we do not see its unsubstantial, passing nature—we do not keep our eyes fixed on Heaven, where Christ is, seated at the right hand of the Father.[10]

A retreat is the reorientation of ourselves towards the supernatural order—towards reality. And such reorientation is always painful. It means looking at the ways in which we conform to the world, or are tempted to, and the reasons for that in ourselves. Is it pride? Is it sloth? Is it timidity? A desire for security? What are the reasons, day by day, that we don't detach ourselves from the world?

If we see the word wrongly, failing to possess a Catholic vision of it, it is not merely that we're stupid or reason wrongly—it's not just error. We are in error and blind because it *suits us* to be. Because we make up a world which suits our own sinful, disordered passions. And the first stage in acquiring a grasp of reality is examination of conscience, confession, and planning; in order to replace those disordered passions—and actual vices—with virtues.

Notes

1. Luigi Cardinal Lambruschini (1776–1854), Prefect of the Congregations of Rites, and of Studies, Vice-Dean of the Sacred College. He had been Gregory XVI's Secretary of State, and was thought to be the most popular 'conservative' candidate in the conclave that finally elected the 'liberal' candidate Cardinal Ferretti as Pope Pius IX.
2. Blessed Pope Pius IX issued the Encyclical *Ubi Primum* on 2 Feb 1849, signed at Gaeta, the document which paved the way for the proclamation of the doctrine of the Immaculate Conception in 1854 (see endnote 5).
3. Pius IX, Apostolic Constitution *Ineffabilis Deus*, 8th Dec. 1854. *"Declaramus, pronuntiamus et definimus doctrinam quae tenet beatissimam Virginem Mariam in primo instanti suae conceptionis fuisse singulari Omnipotentis Dei gratia et privilegio, intuitu meritorum Christi Jesu Salvatoris humani generis, ab omni originalis culpae labe praeservatam immunem, esse a Deo revelatam, atque idcirco ab omnibus fidelibus firmiter constanterque credendam."* Cf. Denz., n. 1641.
4. L. Cardinal Lambruschini, *A Polemical Treatise on the Immaculate Conception of Mary*, Rome, 1842.
5. Giacomo Filippo Cardinal Fransoni (1775–1856), Cardinal Prefect of the Congregation of Propaganda Fide. Notably, he ordained John Henry Newman to the priesthood in 1847.
6. Father Frederick William Faber, Cong. Orat. (1814–1863), *An Eplanation of the Doctrine and Definition of the Immaculate Conception, with a Meditation* (London: C. Dolman, 1855), p. 3. Fr Cadoc refers to him either as "Father Faber" or "Father Wilfrid"—a reference to his devotion to St Wilfrid, patron of the short-lived religious community Faber founded in Staffordshire upon becoming a Catholic ("The Brothers of the Will of God") before ordination as a Catholic priest and becoming the Founder-Provost of the London Oratory. Faber's remains lie in front of the altar in St Wilfrid's Chapel in the London Oratory.
7. For the avoidance of confusion: Fr Cadoc uses the older English "worship", not for *latria* (worship due only to God), but for *dulia* (veneration of the Saints), and in this case *hyperdulia* (the veneration of Our Blessed Lady in particular).
8. Luke 1:46
9. Namely in the Priory in Chelmsford; Marian devotion is a particularly notable characteristic of all Norbertine life and spirituality.
10. Cf. Colossians 3:1–2

Opening Prayer

Jesu, vivens in Maria.

O Jesus, who dost live in Mary,
come and live in Thy servants;
in the spirit of Thine own holiness,
in the fullness of Thy power,
in the reality of Thy virtues,
in the perfection of Thy ways,
in the communion of Thy mysteries.
Have Thou dominion over every adverse power,
in Thine own Spirit, to the glory of the Father. Amen.

Second Conference

Now, in the first talk, I didn't really speak about the Immaculate Conception at all. I spoke rather about the historical event of the definition of the doctrine as an article of faith. What then *is* the Immaculate Conception? It is the doctrine which holds—I quote *Ineffabilis Deus*—"that the most Blessed Virgin Mary, in the first instant of her conception... in view of the merits of Jesus Christ... was preserved free from all stain of Original Sin." And the next question to arise, inevitably, is this: What is Original Sin? So again, I do little more than quote. Man in his creation is intended for true union with God in His holiness; a single act of sin is something of such immensity— because of the nature of God's holiness—that it is capable of destroying the human relationship with God, effected by sanctifying grace, that grace which effects *union* with God. Since it is to such a union that man was constituted, man is simply no longer that which he should have been. In him the essence the theologians call "original justice" has been dissolved, and the human passions are no longer subject to the effective control of right reason. He is thus subject to the power of evil: he is within the dominion of the Evil One.

That, clearly, is what we must understand, if we are to grasp the concept of the Immaculate Conception. Now, of course, in a retreat conference, I should not wish to enter into a theological discussion. I simply want to remind you of what you do doubt know. It is:

Firstly, the loss of sanctifying grace, by which man may be truly in union with God. And since that was the purpose of our creation—that we might enter into *that* relationship with God, and attain "theosis", or *divinisation*—Original Sin is that state in which we are no longer what we were intended to be at Creation, in the mind of God. Our constitution as fallen human beings is different. We have lost what our classical theologians, St Thomas, St Anselm, and others, call "original justice". In us, fallen beings, that harmony which is the essence of "original justice" is dissolved, and we have what Thomas calls a "disordered disposition" in which right reason no longer exercises effective control over our passions, our desires. The consequence of this is that we have become part of a realm which is subject to the power of evil. Fallen man is under the dominion of the Evil One.

And so there is a New Creation—a Second Adam and a Second Eve—Jesus and Mary, who effect a more wonderful union with God than that proposed in the first Creation.

So, in brief, the doctrine of the Immaculate Conception refers to TWO things: It refers in the first place to separation from God, the source of all goodness, and therefore to Evil. It refers in the second place to God's overcoming of that, and a restoration—in a way beyond anything that man could have hoped for—of union with God, in the Hypostatic Union and the Immaculate Conception. Even more briefly, the Immaculate Conception is about evil *and* the triumph over it.

And that is why the world needs desperately to have the Immaculate Conception preached to it. It has no notion of evil. It endures evil, but it has no understanding of what it endures. If you ask, in this society we live in, for some example of real evil, it is very unlikely that you will get more than a mouthing of political propaganda—a list of the political opponents our own regime has demonised: Adolf Hitler, Idi Amin, Osama bin Laden. For most people, evil is something not only outside themselves, but outside their society. It is merely the heresy of some other political sect than the one that governs their own society. Now this is something to which we must give thought, if we have a concern for the salvation of souls.

We speak of the Conversion of England; in the nineteenth century (and this retreat seems to have a nineteenth-century themed décor!), that might have meant restoring the Christians of England to the jurisdiction of the Holy See, or perhaps, creating a Catholic confessional State. Now, it decidedly means converting the *pagan* people of England.

Now what do we know about converting folk? Of course, the Church has long experience of this. For more than a millennium and a half, holy men have been wandering over the face of Europe and the Americas; read St Bede's account of Saint Aidan, or of St Boniface,

St Willibrord, and so on. The early modern Jesuits, Capuchins, or later the sons of St Louis-Marie, Sant'Alfonso, or St Paul of the Cross. I mustn't forget San Leonardo![1] Now, fundamental to all of their preaching was what the Evangelicals would call "conviction of sin" — they strove to bring their auditors to an understanding of the power of sin to destroy, of the power of evil in their lives. Evil was not only external to them, but was at work *within them*, and with which they, fallen human beings, wilfully cooperated. *Only then*, knowing the peril they stood in, could they receive the Gospel of Christ — for only then could they know what a Saviour, what *Salvation*, was. "Repent and believe" as Scripture says — and putting them in that order.[2]

What I am speaking of is a reality that needs our attention by virtue of our apostolic vocation — but, of course, if we have regard for our own salvation too. It is an *extreme* situation in which a person *totally* externalises evil and fails to see it at work; at work *often* like a near instant poison; at work in themselves. But in *all* of us, our immune systems are weak by virtue of the process of self-excusation, the relentless search for mitigating circumstances. It is often said nowadays that there is a constant need for conversion — thus, inevitably, constant self-accusation. We have been given not only the Sacrament of Baptism, but also the Sacrament of Penance.

While speaking of the way in which the preaching of the doctrine of the Immaculate Conception calls on us to take seriously the evil of the world and the power of sin at work in us, I must also mention a much neglected matter in much of the present-day Church — the Church's teaching about Apocalyptic. The Immaculate Conception of our Blessed Mother is a prophetic event. It is a *proleptic*—though real and actually accomplished—triumph over evil, by virtue of the Passion and Death of the Lord. And so the mystery will only be finally disclosed to us in the triumph over Antichrist at the Second Coming of the Lord.

Now we back away from this. We have no wish to be identified as arrogant cranks, breathing out impotent fury on a world on which we have appointed *ourselves* to sit in judgement, because it displeases us. We have no desire to be confused with the cranky purveyors of bizarre interpretations of the books of Daniel and Revelation. But Father Faber points to an important phenomenon: the way in which throughout Christian history the saints, and especially the contemplative saints (those most disengaged from worldly life), have taken what he calls "a strange and unexpected interest in the external fortunes of the Church:" the Church which they have seen in *every* age to be in particular peril—"and rightly so!" he says. The Church is always *truly* threatened by the power of evil. "What a lessons is this from these saints," he declares. And they respond to this perceived peril with lives in which a major driving force is the need for intercession *for* the Church—intercession made through, and to, the *Immaculata*, the Co-Redemptrix, the Mediatrix of Grace.

Christopher Dawson, at the very end of his book on the Oxford Movement, points out the presence in that Movement of an "apocalyptic spirit,"[3] as he calls it, which underlay all its early teachings, and which all its converts, I'd add, carried into a receptive Catholic Church. They were not, of course, into calculating times and seasons. But they were quite clear that the afflictions of the Church in all ages were to be read as already partially realised prophecies of the persecutions and mass apostasies of the final age of human history. "It is as though our Lord," says Fr Faber, repeating a commonplace, "would *always* have us longing for His coming."

As Catholics, these men found the appropriate response to this reality in devotion to the *Immaculata*, to her who was destined to crush the head of the Serpent under heel, to her whose arms had been prepared by the Lord for battle. Fr Faber perceived every increase in devotion to her, by the Church and by its individual sons and daughters, as preparation for the Church's final conflict. After all, in Mary, in the Immaculate Conception, there was the promise of victory.

Fr Faber, among many others, knew precisely what form that devotion should take. Because it was just in 1842—as it happened—that the manuscript of St Louis-Marie de Montfort's treatise *On True Devotion to the Blessed Virgin* was discovered after more than a century during which it had lain hidden. Now, it is not my intention to speak much of the teaching of St Louis-Marie. I should, even had I the time, be afraid to do so; because, despite the simplicity of style, I am now speaking of one of the most profound teachers of the Church in the modern age, and I am intimidated. (Open brackets!) That does not mean that you should be: I am certain the *practice* of his doctrine will open the way to its meaning for you. (Close brackets!) All I will say is this: his newly discovered teaching was perfectly suited to the age of the definition of the Immaculate Conception. He possessed a deep understanding of Mary's identity as the Immaculate Conception, as one who was never for an instant subject to the power of Evil. And the consequence of that is her ability to give victory in the conflict of Good and

Evil—what the Book of Genesis calls the "enmities between her seed and the seed of the Evil One."[4] This was founded on an appreciation of the scope of her Divine Maternity; his understanding was that the Holy Spirit produces Jesus Christ in His members through Mary, and that we are truly by Baptism and Confirmation the 'Seed of Mary'—destined for conflict, but victorious conflict. He prophesied the victories of the last age of human history. He knew that—and I quote the *True Devotion*—"the formation and education of the great saints who shall come at the end of the world are reserved for her"—for Mary Immaculate.[5]

It is a great defect of the Church in our age that it lacks the courage to preach Apocalyptic. For the "types and foreshadowings" of the age of Antichrist (as Blessed John Henry Newman called them) are real dangers to the Church; souls are lost by them. And so we must declare their evil character; but always with a declaration of faith in the *Immaculata* to overcome and crush them.

Notes

1 Fr Cadoc often refers to Italian saints in Italian – here Saint Alphosus de' Liguori, and Saint Leonard of Port Maurice (one of his favourites).
2 Cf. Mark 1:15.
3 Christopher Dawson (1889–1970), *The Spirit of the Oxford Movement* (London: Sheed and Ward, 1933), p. 126.
4 Cf. Genesis 3:15.
5 St Louis-Marie Grignon de Montfort, *A Treatise on the True Devotion to the Blessed Virgin*, Translated by Fr F. W. Faber (London: Burns and Lambert, 1863), p. 20.

Opening Prayer

Jesu, vivens in Maria.

O Jesus, who dost live in Mary,
come and live in Thy servants;
in the spirit of Thine own holiness,
in the fullness of Thy power,
in the reality of Thy virtues,
in the perfection of Thy ways,
in the communion of Thy mysteries.
Have Thou dominion over every adverse power,
in Thine own Spirit, to the glory of the Father. Amen.

Third Conference

HAVE SPOKEN SOMEWHAT—IN the first lecture—of the historical event of the definition of the Immaculate Conception, on Friday 8 December 1854. I moved on to say—in the second lecture—what the doctrine was about. I now want to say something to help place it in context, to explain something of its place in Christian doctrine and Christian life.

There is a pernicious attitude to *Marianism*—to Marian doctrine and devotion—which we need to root out. It has always been around among Protestants, but it has in recent decades penetrated the Church itself. It goes, I think, with a strange notion that Protestantism represents a basic version of Christianity, while Catholicism is constituted by this, *plus* some perhaps attractive and desirable additions—*adiaphora*, or things not really necessary. In a Catholic version of this theory we hear of Protestant beliefs being merely *incomplete*. Nonsense! Protestantism is not merely incomplete—its error penetrates it all the way through, in thought and in practice. And Marian doctrine and devotion is no ornamental addition to Christianity: it is an integral part of it, and without it we cannot understand the *rest* of Revelation. Because without Marianism, the human beings to whom God addresses this Revelation, and their necessary participation and cooperation in the saving events, are ignored. The Christian Revelation becomes a sound without hearers—does it exist?—or a play that is never performed—never becoming a drama—which exists only in potency.

The point is: Mary's attentiveness to the Word of God, "like the eyes of a servant on the hand of her Lord,"[1] not just listening, but "putting the Word into practice,"[2] and willingly and actively cooperating in what God declares,—that He wills our Salvation, His union with the ones He loves—this is an integral part of the Revelation: *its realisation*. And Marian devotion is no subjective luxury, as it has often been depicted; it is the source of a living power that we *need* to conduct our Christian lives. If there is any charity in us, if we have any care for the salvation of souls, we need to communicate this to people: it is necessary for their salvation. The calendar I nicked from the Calefactory for my office, with nice pictures of medieval churches, says on each page, "Britain needs Fatima!"— Just so.

As soon as we begin to think a little about the Immaculate Conception, we begin to see how integral Marian doctrine is to the whole structure of Christian thought. We call the Immaculate Conception "the dawn of the world's redemption";[3] very pretty— dawns are beautiful—but no, that's inadequate. It is, rather, Redemption already realised and visible, in the person of the Blessed Virgin. Here, *already*, the power of evil has been broken in her who is our Mother, *and* our union with the Divine has *already* been realised. No, it is not dawn: it is full daylight.

Put it another way: the ending of the story has been declared to us in the Immaculate Conception. It only remains to see how beautifully the most Blessed Trinity tells that story, and to see the wonders along the way, in the earthly and eternal lives of Jesus, Mary, and the Saints. But, with regard to those wonders along the way, they take their *origin* from the Immaculate Conception. Father Faber's words: "The Immaculate Conception is the foundation of all the other mysteries of Jesus and Mary, and of the Church, and of the Seven Sacraments."

As soon as we begin to think of this, we can see what Father Wilfrid means. The Immaculate Conception is the fitting preparation for the Incarnation. In it, for example, we see how it came about that Mary gave her *willing consent* to the Incarnation. And what a revelation of God's disposition towards us *that* is. He *required* that willing consent from His creature, because He *loves*, and could not seek anything but a free response in love.

In the Immaculate Conception we see the preparation of the willing Bride of the Holy Spirit. And again, God Himself—God the Holy Spirit—is revealed to us: from our perception of the Bride, we see the Spouse Himself. Mary is the created image of the Holy Spirit, eternally predestined and formed to be His Bride, then sanctified by Him. But that thought of Mary as the Spouse of the Holy Spirit rushes us beyond the Annunciation to the great *Marian* mystery of Pentecost and the formation of the Church: in it we see Mary, no longer the hesitant young woman of the Annunciation, but the woman calling confidently on her Spouse, the Holy Spirit, so that her Son might be born again, and have His life, in His disciples; this is St Louis-Marie's teaching, that I spoke of briefly in the last lecture. In the Immaculate Conception we have the origins of the Church: Mary being prepared to become the Mother of the Mystical Body, which we see born of her at Pentecost.

I'm only attempting to illustrate briefly the point that, as soon as we begin to meditate on the Immaculate Conception, there opens before us the whole of the Christian Revelation. And the Immaculate Conception is the natural, the *right* way to enter into the Christian Revelation, because it is the fountain from which the other mysteries of our Faith flow, and their meaning and end (our freedom from the captivity of sin and our ultimate union with God) are already clear to us. In the Immaculate Conception, we have, as it were, come in at the entrance and seen in outline the plan of the whole structure.

What I say also, is that if we *do* use the doctrine of the Immaculate Conception to lead us into the Christian Revelation, we have a great advantage: we go forward with Mary, with someone who has already received it, and we receive it perfectly; she not merely understood it, but lived it, and to perfection. And that reception of the Christian Revelation by Mary is, as I have already said, an immensely important *part* of the Revelation. It tells us what the coming of Christ actually *does* in a human life: how, for us, the Redemption effected by the Incarnation and the Paschal Mystery actually works out and achieves its purpose in us.

Let's make a basic point: the Incarnation of the Second Person of the Blessed Trinity has taken place so that we may draw close to God, and actually enter into union with Him. Closeness, in the spiritual realm, Our Holy Father Augustine says somewhere, is similitude.[4] The Second Person of the Blessed Trinity has become one *like us*, so that we can become *like Him*. The one who has most perfectly attained this is Mary. In her life we see the process of our Redemption revealed, because we see her similitude to her Son. We cannot actually contemplate Mary *without* contemplating Jesus at the same time. What I am saying is that this similitude is an essential element in the Christian Revelation. And the Immaculate Conception is—and again, I am merely quoting Father Wilfrid—the primary revelation of Mary's similitude to Jesus, because in this she received the fullness of grace that made it possible, indeed, already partly accomplished. And this similitude to Jesus is the revelation of what the process of salvation *is*, up close.

Mary is most like her Son in His struggle against evil, against sin. Of course, for our Saviour and His Mother, that *was* a struggle with something external to them. Nevertheless, that struggle was far more extreme than ours, and accompanying Mary in that struggle is always immensely constructive for us. It was so much more intense for Mary, precisely by virtue of her Immaculate Conception: she was always aware of the true horror of sin. Her own closeness to God, springing from her deliverance from Original Sin, and her *actual* sinlessness, allowed her always to perceive clearly the terrifying nature of the sin around her, destroying those whom she *loved*. And so we learn courage from her in facing evil. We learn too the inevitability, the unavoidable nature, of painful conflict with evil. It was her very love that inflicted the worst blows on her, particularly at the foot of the Cross. The more we advance in charity, the greater the struggle. And it is a relentless struggle! From the prophecy of St Simeon, Mary is constantly facing into a renewal of battle with evil, but she is always willing—in love—to endure the next torment that comes upon her. From Mary we learn the nature of our struggle against evil, and, especially reflecting on the fullness of grace given in the Immaculate Conception, the way in which we can *survive* the struggle: by a total dependence on God's grace, never on our own capacity.

One might go on speaking of the various similitudes of Mary to Jesus: obedience to the Father, so different from our own indulgence of, and pandering to, our own perverse and destructive wills; or again, the hiddenness of so much of her life, so different from us, constantly trying to thrust ourselves on the world and display the remarkable nature of our contribution. But, that is not my point for the moment. I leave it to you to draw it out in meditation. Rather, I want to speak of Mary's similitude to Jesus in general.

In us, similitude to Jesus is the process of salvation, the means by which it comes about. In Mary, it is that too, but more: and that 'more' is used for us. In Mary, it is the source of her glories. In her similarity to Him who is to become her Son—the Second Person of the Trinity—and, specifically, in His perfect obedience to the Father (in *that* similarity), she is able to freely consent to become the Mother of God. In her similarity to her Son in His love for us, she is able to intercede for us and become the Dispensatrix of all God's graces. In her similarity to Jesus in His willingness to suffer and die out of love for us and for His Father, she is able to endure suffering her whole life long, and stand at the foot of the Cross, and participate in our Redemption: she is Co-Redemptrix.

In us, similitude to Jesus is not *just* the process of our salvation—it is also our Christian hope. If we will share Christ's Passion—St Paul tells us—then we shall also share His Resurrection and triumph.[5] The same is true of Mary; but it is far greater glory in the case of Mary. We are speaking now of the fourth and fifth Glorious Mysteries of the Holy Rosary: her Assumption and Coronation. She, who in her earthly life possessed such an elevated, perfect similitude to her Son—far beyond that of all the other faithful who would come after her—is now attended with a glory beyond theirs, which lies in the nature of her union with God and her eternal participation in her Son's Kingship.

Notes

1. Cf. Psalm 123:2.
2. Cf. James 1:25.
3. Unsurprisingly, citations for this are hard to find. Sometimes, however, Mary is characterised as the Dawn, and Christ the Day. Cf. Pope St John Paul II, *Prayer* at the homage to the *Immaculata* at the Piazza di Spagna, Rome, 8 December 1999; *Angelus*, Monday 8 December 2003, 1. Fr Cadoc's love of Marian hymns may also be a clue; he may have been thinking of the first stanza of this hymn by Fr E Caswall Cong. Orat. (1814–1878), included in the English translation of the Roman Breviary for 8 December: "Holy light on earth's horizon, / star of hope to fallen man, / light amid a world of shadows, / dawn of God's redemptive plan, / chosen from eternal ages, / thou alone of all our race, / by thy Son's atoning merits / wast conceived in perfect grace."
4. Saint Augustine actually treats this in various places: *De Genesi ad litteram liber imperfectus* 16, 55–62; *De diversis quaestionibus* LXXXIII, 51.4, 74; *De Trinitate* VII, 6, 12 ; *Quaestiones in Heptateucham* V, 44; *Retractationes* I, 26. (Cited by R A Markus, *"Imago and Similitudo in Augustine"*, Revue d'Etudes Augustiniennes et Patristiques, 1963, Vol.10 2–3, p. 131).
5. Cf. Romans 6:8, 2 Timothy 2:11.

Opening Prayer

Jesu, vivens in Maria.

O Jesus, who dost live in Mary,
come and live in Thy servants;
in the spirit of Thine own holiness,
in the fullness of Thy power,
in the reality of Thy virtues,
in the perfection of Thy ways,
in the communion of Thy mysteries.
Have Thou dominion over every adverse power,
in Thine own Spirit, to the glory of the Father. Amen.

Fourth Conference

s we come towards the end of our retreat, let us again ask St Herman Joseph to help us. We pray that whatever we have gained in increased attention and devotion to our Blessed Lady during these days of retreat may not be lost because of the tasks and distractions of our daily lives. Rather, may it serve to encourage us to turn consciously to her more and more, so that we may be enabled to turn more and more of our lives into offerings to her and to her Divine Son. *St Herman Joseph, pray for us.*

The Immaculate Conception: of course, the words—as I have said before—are rich in meaning. There is the *doctrine* of the Immaculate Conception, and there is Mary, who (it was reiterated at Lourdes) *is* the Immaculate Conception. I have been urging you, and myself, through the medium of these conferences, to preach both the *doctrine* and the *person*. To *preach*, that is, both in what we say, and in the whole conduct of our lives.

Having spoken a great deal about the doctrine, I want now to speak more about the person. Having spoken about what we may *say*, I want to speak more about how we *live*. Or, to combine both points, I want to say that *we are to live with the Immaculata*.

Perhaps I might say that I am urging you to a devotion to Our Lady of Loreto and Our Lady of Walsingham. I am urging you—and again, myself—to live in constant proximity to Mary, *in her house*, within her household, being supported and nourished by her, looked after by her, learning to be like her and her Divine Son. And I am wondering what that is like, what that might mean for us.

And my first thought is: Can we practise this devotion? Do we dare? We, with the knowledge of our past sins, our habitual sins, our fear of future sins? Do we dare go to the door of the Holy House? Do you know that famous depiction by Caravaggio of Our Lady of Loreto, in the Church of Sant'Agostino in the Via della Scrofa? It is of this: the battered pilgrims to Loreto approaching the door of the Holy House to be received by the Madonna, the Holy Child in her arms.[1] Do we dare go in with those other *viatores*?

Yes, we know we can, because of Mary's love for us: we know her as the Refuge of Sinners. Which means, not that sin does not matter to her, but that she effectively helps us in our daily battle against sin. How does this come about?

Take the worst case—sin already committed. We are already defeated, depressed and discouraged about sinning, and willing to lie there, deciding it's useless to struggle. It really is enough to look up at Mary, in genuine, committed love, rather than give way to a proud, self-indulgent gloominess and misery.

Look up, and ask for her pardon and *her* word to her Son for you. Ask at once. Promise yourself to perform the next thing you do in such a way as to give the greatest possible joy to her and to Jesus. Do not remain for a *single minute* in the state of sin. Ask for forgiveness immediately. Of course, we'll acknowledge our sin in our next confession. But meanwhile, we act and conduct ourselves in an attitude of confidence in the power of the intercession of the *Immaculata*, and be saved from falling deeper into sin. We can have that confidence, I believe, if we are among those habitually trying to have a consciousness of the presence of Mary. It's in this way that the *Immaculata* comes to our aid, even when it seems that it is already too late, lifting us up as soon as we have begun to sink.

If, on the other hand, we are habitually and seriously trying to fight against sin—let's think more positively—and are staunch in this endeavour, the *Immaculata* comes to our help even before we fall. If we are habitually trying to live in closeness to the *Immaculata*—the one who has already conquered sin—we can see the danger approaching. And St Bernard says we must go to her when conscious of trouble and danger. Put aside pride: behave like a child, and run to the arms of your Mother, confident that there, nothing bad can happen to you. Indeed it can't: an earthly mother cannot always protect the child who trusts her; but the *Immaculata* can.

If we are persistent in resisting sin, by trusting in the *Immaculata*, we will eventually perceive ourselves to be, as it were, under her direction in the struggle.

Remember that Ferdinand II made the *Immaculata* "Generalissima" of the imperial armies.[2] She'll have us in the right place, to avoid unnecessary danger.

She'll have us able and *armed* for the fight: there is the *grace* she gives us. That grace is what is *good* within us, and what gives us strength; and this is what she gives. Our consciousness of what is *evil* in us—that which comes from ourselves—is limited, and that is for our good. Saint Maximilian Kolbe remarks: "The evil that we see in ourselves is not all of it; the *Immaculata* allows us to see only a little, so that we do not forget who we are, in and of ourselves."[3] And so, to put it in a word, our morale is kept up.

So far, I have been speaking of the negative aspect—the struggle *against* sin. That struggle is, in the first place, what our belief in the doctrine of the Immaculate Conception calls us to. It calls us to take part in that triumph over sin which is already shown in the Immaculate Conception to be possible, indeed, certain. But the doctrine of the Immaculate Conception is also about the restoration of sanctifying grace. Mary now bestows all the graces of sanctification, from those given to *her*. But how is this actually realised in our lives? What is the activity going on within the Holy House of Nazareth, of Loreto, of Walsingham, to which we have come? Well, we are learning. That's what's going on. We are learning that in order to become holy, we must follow Christ, be conformed to Christ, and strive for that about which I spoke in the last conference: similitude to Christ. That is our fundamental lesson to be learned. And who can possible teach this to us better than the *Immaculata*, in whom that similitude was perfect?

Or, let me put it another, better way: Through whom did Christ come into the world? We can answer easily, thinking of what Scripture records: the Annunciation, the birth at Bethlehem. But birth is not the end of

Fourth Conference

maternity. We must think on to the years of the Holy Infancy. Who *raised* the Incarnate God, to whom we are to acquire similitude? To whom was He obedient? His character, as Incarnate God, by *nurture* entirely, though nature is another matter, was given to Him primarily by His Mother. And *we* have to ask and allow the Mother of God to bring *us* up after the pattern of Jesus Christ; but more, thinking again of the Holy House, in the *company* of Jesus Christ, as a loved brother and one who we know—as Mary did from the prophecy of Saint Simeon—is to suffer for us, die for us.

This notion of Mary *forming* the Incarnate God, as she forms those who allow her to be a Mother to them, strikes me as interesting; because it explains, I think, what is meant when theology speaks of the "fittingness" of the Immaculate Conception of her who was to be the Mother of the Word Incarnate.[4] Because she was not just to give birth to Him; she was to *fashion* Him in His upbringing. The Immaculate Conception was more than merely *fitting* in the sense of *appropriate,* or *becoming*. It was *necessary,* for the Incarnation to achieve its purpose; Mary *had* to be Immaculate to make the Incarnate Word be what *He* had to be. God's seeking of Mary's permission for the Incarnation lasted, I think, much longer than that moment before the uttering of her "fiat", so beautifully described by Saint Bernard.[5]

Now, whether we see Mary conformed to Christ, or the Incarnate God conformed to His creature (He, in any case—it is lovely to reflect—was conformed to His creature in His physical appearance), it doesn't really matter. We are speaking of similitude. Mary teaches us similitude to Christ, which is also similitude to her. The question *we* ask is: What is the content of that similitude? What is it that we are to be brought up to *be*? What is it that we are to learn?

Well, the retreat is coming to an end, and I can hardly start trying now to answer the question, "what is the life of the Christian like? In what does it consist?" Let me speak only of the foundation: the foundation of Mary's life—the Immaculate Conception.

I don't, of course, by "foundation" mean her life's temporal beginning. Remember that what she said at Lourdes was *not* that she was immaculately conceived, but that she *was* the Immaculate Conception: that is her *identity*. From the first moment of her existence, Mary is perfect, radiantly pure, and immaculate. That means, among other things, that the roots of her being and of her life are completely and utterly in keeping with the divine order. She is what the Divine Wisdom, the Word of the Father, intended the human creature to be. That is to say that, from the very first moment, her life is unreservedly, absolutely and perfectly directed towards God. That is what the Divine Wisdom intended, because that reflects the internal life of the Most Blessed Trinity—the perfect love of the Persons for each other. It is this unreserved, absolute, perfect direction of life towards God that has been stymied in us by Original Sin. The process of our sanctification is the re-realising of it. That is what Mary is fundamentally attempting to do, in her motherly care for, and instruction of, us.

The process of education is fundamentally made up of two things. Firstly, imitation. I am not in the business of transferring gobbets of information about European History from my mind to that of my students: I'm in the business of getting them to think as I do as an historian, of getting them to imitate me in that respect.

And the other element is getting them to please me, by submitting the right paper, the right theses.

If we want to please Mary our Mother—because she loves us—we must imitate her in that unreserved, absolute, perfect direction of our lives towards God. That is to say, never directing them towards the satisfaction of our own misguided desires for ourselves; never directing them to other creatures, except out of the love He was for them. And we must always seize the present moment to try to give Mary our Mother that consolation and joy of seeing her children *in hac lacrimarum valle*[6] overcoming their sadness and misery, and taking the way she has marked out for them. That way is the *Reditus*—the Return. God's creation is a great act of His self-giving, a pouring-out of His light and life beyond Himself, so that there may be real "others" who will love Him and return to Him. That is the meaning of the mystery of the Assumption: the mystery in which *we*, in this Order dedicated to the *Assumpta*,[7] have taken upon ourselves to immerse ourselves.

Notes

1. Caravaggio (1571–1610), *Madonna dei Pellegrini,* or *Madonna di Loreto* (1604–1606). It hangs in the Cavalletti chapel of the Church of Sant'Agostino in Rome.
2. Ferdinand II (1578–1637), Holy Roman Emperor from 1619–1637, made this declaration to Our Lady during the Thirty Years War (as did Elector Maximilian I of Bavaria), giving thanks to her by crowning her at Mariazell in June 1621, vowing to expel all heretics from Bohemia. Our Lady's title of *Generalissima* of the imperial armies and patroness of the Hapsburgs (typical of the *Pietas Austriaca* so beloved of Fr Cadoc) was renewed at Mariazell several times, including in 1676 by Emperor Leopold I, who addressed prayer to the Virgin of Mariazell in which he renewed the title.
3. St Maximilian Kolbe OFM Conv. (1894–1941), Letter to Brother X, in: P. J. Domański, *Co dzien ze sw. Maksymilianem* (Niepokalanów 1994), p. 135.
4. On the much-used word "fitting" to describe the Immaculate Conception (even mentioned by Blessed Pope Pius IX in *Ineffabilis Deus*), we may simply mention that it was said by Saint Anselm (Treatise on the Virginal Conception), and is repeated in the Catechism of the Catholic Church, CCC 722.
5. Fr Cadoc certainly refers to Saint Bernard of Clairvaux, *Homily in Praise of the Virgin Mother, Homily* 4, 8–9.
6. "In this valley of tears" – words from the *Salve Regina*.
7. Our Lady is celebrated on 15th August (Solemnity of her Assumption) by all Norbertines as the Patroness of the Premonstratensian Order (*Patrona Ordinis nostri*).

Appendix

I have now finished the series of conferences, and I add a mere appendix, on the retreat conferences that it crossed my mind to give when the Prior first asked me to speak. I thought of speaking about the life of Our Holy Father Norbert, and the early history of our own Order, but abandoned the idea at once, fearing that you would have a series of lectures on twelfth-century religious history, rather than retreat conferences.

In truth, though, the choice probably did not matter. It would, in essence, have been the same subject matter: the need to take seriously the evil that lies hidden within us, and the triumph over it won by the acquisition of similitude to Christ.

Think, for example, of the two accounts of Our Holy Father's conversion: that of the Benedictine monk, Herman, in which Norbert encounters the realities of a sin-infected world in the high politics of the age of the Emperor Henry V, and dedicates himself to confronting that evil by conformity to Christ in his ministry of preaching; or, the account given in the *Vitae* (A and B): the thunderstorm and voice the young nobleman heard, rebuking evil in his *own* life, and his recollection of the words of the psalmist: "Turn aside from evil and do good;"[1] Norbert's words: "Lord, what do you want me to do?;"[2] and the story, thereafter, of Our Holy Father as an apostolic preacher.

In *Vita* A, we hear the context of his preaching: in the first place, the call to his hearers to overcome evil in their lives with penance—that is, similitude to Christ in His sufferings. And then, the instauration—at Prémontré, at Cappenberg, at Ilbenstadt, and so on—of a way of life constructed to produce similitude to Christ. And might we not think too of the frequent accounts of exorcisms in the Vitae? And this story— well, I love the 26th chapter of *Vita* B—of the one novice who was "less devout in his confession, frivolous in speech, restless in his behaviour, inconstant in his practices, tepid in prayer, neglectful in obedience, and dissolute in all things," the *Vita* explains…[3]

You see the point. The life of Our Holy Father—and the lives of those who followed him—are really just explications, unfoldings, of the meaning of that single act wrought by the Holy Trinity at the first instant of Mary's life—the Immaculate Conception—the crushing of evil, the establishment by grace of similitude to Christ. Better, they are the historical realisation of this.

We, wretched, awful as we are, want to be called the sons of those holy men and women. May the mystery of the Immaculate Conception, in some way, unfold itself in our lives.

Our consolation is that Mary our Mother *loves us* very much, and *wants that to happen*, very much.

Appendix

Well … *De Maria numquam satis*[4]… but that will have to be enough for now.

Notes

1. Psalm 34:14.
2. *Vita* B, II, 7. Cf. Acts 9:6.
3. Fr Cadoc went on to explain that Ch. 26 of Vita B describes this false novice, an Englishman (!), as the one who ran off with the money donated by a poor convert. The *Vita* says: "Thus that deceptive fraud and minister of the devil, knowing in his heart that they were poor, increased the poverty of the poor of Christ, who suspected nothing, to such a degree that nothing remained for them to procure supplies for a day. What does this mean? First they had to be tested in regard to bodily food, they who had heard that the possessors of the kingdom of heaven are those who it is clear have become poor, not as to material wealth but as to poverty of spirit. They had to be tested in smaller things in order to learn to stand firm in the storms and confusion which they had to face as events will show in what follows." (*Vita* B, XXVI, 56).
4. "Of Mary one can never say enough." Words attributed to St Bernard of Clairvaux.

www.ingramcontent.com/pod-product-compliance
Lightning Source LLC
Chambersburg PA
CBHW032113040426
42337CB00040B/549